Family Tree

MEMORY KEEPER

Family Tree
MEMORY KEEPER

YOUR WORKBOOK
for Family History, Stories & Genealogy

FROM THE EDITORS OF
FAMILY TREE MAGAZINE

ALLISON DOLAN   DIANE HADDAD

ft
FAMILY
TREE
BOOKS

Table of Contents

VI. RELATIVES IN THE SERVICE
84

Honor ancestors who served in the military or held down the home front during times of war by exploring their experiences and recording them here.

VII. RELATIVES MAKING NEWS
100

Record any newsworthy family moments.

VIII. PLACES
112

Learn about and commemorate your family's journeys—their orgins and the places where they settled.

IX. FAMILY RECIPES
138

Foods evoke strong memories of special times with family. Here's a place to record those recipes and recollections.

X. IMPORTANT DATES
162

Remember birthdays, anniversaries, and other special family dates by writing them on this perpetual calendar.

XI. REFERENCE GUIDE
188

Get the resources and references you need to start discovering, preserving, and celebrating your family's past.

Introduction

Over time most of us feel the pull to the past: Three-quarters of Americans are either interested in or are actively tracing their family trees. That's because we instinctively know that our ancestors' experiences, tribulations, and successes created the families we know today. The shared celebrations, stories, sayings, and beliefs passed from one generation to the next give families a sense of identity and a feeling of closeness. We try to understand our loved ones and ourselves by understanding our ancestors' lives.

In this book, you'll find a place to record your family's story and advice to help you discover new information about your family's past. Write your immediate family's names and special memories in chapter one and other relatives' names, life dates, and places of residence on the family information sheets in chapter two to get started. Then you'll find space to enclose letters, certificates, and other mementos; pages for photos and stories about those photographed; recipe pages for favorite family dishes; and pages to save family stories, news clippings, military service details, and much more. A blank line at the top of each form provides space to record family names.

Whether you've vaguely wondered about your family history or you've already begun to look for information, this book will help you gain new insight into your heritage and preserve your family's unique legacy.

10 STEPS TO DISCOVERING YOUR FAMILY HISTORY

Maybe you're curious about your family's past, but you don't know how to find out about it. Don't worry—getting started isn't difficult. These ten steps show you how to start with information you know or can easily learn, and then you can move on to resources at libraries.

1. Talk to relatives.

Interviewing your family members is one of the first steps to discovering your family history. It's also the step people most often regret not taking after a beloved relative passes away. Maybe you think there's no one left to interview, or you're reluctant to call Great-aunt Mary and pepper her with questions.

Take advantage of the opportunity to ask relatives about your family history. Not only will you get to know a family member, you'll learn valuable genealogical information and hear family stories you can pass on to future generations. Use the tips in chapter three to make your interviews a smooth process.

2. Record names, dates, and places on a family tree chart.

Write down what you know so you can see what you don't know yet. Start with a simple five-generation ancestor chart. You'll record ancestors' names on the chart, as well as birth, marriage, and death dates and places. Use a family group sheet to record information about each nuclear family.

3. Search for letters, certificates, and other family papers.

A lot of family information may already be in your own or a relative's home in what are commonly called "home sources." Look through the boxes in your attic, basement, and closets for old letters, diaries, military papers, the family Bible, birth and marriage certificates, photos, and other heirlooms. Offer to help family members search their homes, too. Examine each one for family history clues—names; dates of births, marriages, and deaths; migrations; military service; etc. Write down everything you find on the genealogy charts and in this book.

4. Look for family information in census and vital records.

After you gather all the family facts you can from relatives and home sources, it's time to check out some basic genealogical records: censuses and vital records (birth, marriage, and death certificates).

Federal censuses, taken every ten years since 1790, give different information about your ancestors depending on which census you're looking at. You might learn their address, age, birthplace, marital status, immigration date, country of origin, occupation, citizenship status, ability to read, and more. Check every census during each ancestor's lifetime.

Birth, marriage, and death certificates—collectively called vital records—are basic genealogical records that can give you those dates to help you fill in blanks on your ancestor charts. They're available in most places starting in the late 1800s or early 1900s. Vital records also can tell you the person's place of residence and, even better, parents' names. See chapter two to learn how to find census and vital records.

5. Flesh out family stories.
Now that you have a lot of names and dates, it's time to flesh those out with information from other records. You might learn about your Civil War ancestor's experiences in his pension file, for example, or read about a great-uncle's business in the local paper. In court records, you can learn about lawsuits, custody hearings and other cases your relatives were party to. We'll help you find these records with tips inside the various chapters of this book.

6. Gather family photographs.
Get your old photo albums out of the closet. Each image captures a particular moment in your family's past—and tells their story in ways words alone can't. For this book, you'll want to collect a selection of favorite photographs that best represents your family's story. That includes special occasions and everyday moments. Ask your relatives to share their photos, too—especially pictures of older and past generations—so you can save the stories behind those images. Use the pages in chapter four to record key details and memories for each photo; you'll also find advice for preserving your pictures and identifying unknown images.

7. Explore your heritage.
Whether your ancestors came from Asia, Europe, Africa, Australia, South America, or North America, you'll want to learn more about their lives in the old country. If you have a family story suggesting which ancestor immigrated, you have a head start; otherwise, work backward until you identify the immigrant. More than 40 percent of Americans have a relative who came through Ellis Island, and you can search its records for free at *<www.ellisisland.org>*. For records of New York arrivals prior to Ellis Island's opening in 1892, try *<www.castlegarden.org>*. Of course, your ancestor could have come through many other ports, from Boston to San Francisco. If they came by boat, you can find the ship's manifest. Find out more in chapter eight.

8. Learn about your family's hometowns.
The places we live are part of our identities, from the hometown sports teams we root for to the traditions we adhere to. The same is true of our ancestors: Perhaps your great-grandmother is remembered for the sauerbraten recipe she brought with her from Germany, or maybe you know your kin were among the Virginia line of the Williams family, not the Massachusetts Williamses. Even beyond those basic geographic ties, the communities your relatives lived in are the key to unlocking your family history. That's because historical records are kept at the local level. Just as you'd you go to a county office to apply for a marriage license or file a will, your ancestors' key life events were documented by counties and towns in the United States. So be sure to look for and keep track of your ancestors' hometowns. The maps in chapter eight will help you plot the places your family lived; use stickers or a marker to mark those locations. You'll also find pages to record details and stories about ancestral places of residence.

9. Save—and share—your discoveries.
Documenting and discovering your family history is a personally gratifying experience, to be sure. But it's also a gift to present to future generations of your family. So don't keep this book and the family stories and information you uncover to yourself. You might want to make copies of heirloom photos and documents to share with relatives. If you're more ambitious, consider creating a keepsake gift, such as a cookbook of heritage recipes or a CD of family photos, to give each family at your annual reunion or holiday gathering. (Turn to chapter eleven CD-creation instructions.) To preserve documents and heirlooms you don't keep in this book, you'll want to use archival-friendly storage supplies—find a list of purveyors in chapter eleven. Be sure to back up any electronic files (digital photos, downloaded document images) and store them in a separate location, such as a safe-deposit box or another relative's house, to guard against computer crashes, floods, fires, or other disasters.

10. Get extra assistance.
Once you've completed this book, you may discover you're hungry to learn more about your family's past. Or perhaps you've found you'll need to do some more digging in order to flesh out certain sections. The final chapter of this book is filled with resources and advice that will help you do just that. You'll find Web sites and publications to explore, software for family tree tracking, sources for archival-safe storage supplies and snazzy family tree wall charts, DNA testing resources, reference charts, and organizations you can consult for further assistance.

I

Our Family

In this section, you'll record information about the immediate family you grew up in and your spouse, children, and grandchildren. These are usually the family members you know the best and have spent the most time with. There is also space for photographs of the special people in your life.

Your family's identity is inextricably linked with your last name. It's fun to find out what your name means, which you can do at *<learn.ancestry.com>* or in the books listed in the Reference Guide. These resources also can tell you where on the globe people with your last name often came from (which, of course, doesn't necessarily mean that's where *your* family came from). Write down what you learn on one of the Family Name pages provided in this section. (You can use the others to record notes and stories about your mother's maiden name and other family surnames.) Next you can add all of the family stories you have heard about your

name. Keep in mind that many families have stories of being related to famous historical figures, without anything to prove or disprove the legend. If your family has such a tale, write it down in this section and note that it's a story. You can use the advice in this book to look for records that'll confirm the story, or reveal a different tale.

Some families changed their names over many generations, often to sound more "American" after immigrating to the United States. Don't fall for the myth that some Ellis Island official changed your immigrant ancestor's name. That's actually not true: Ellis Island officials just made sure the name the person gave matched what was on the ship's list of passengers. It's likely, too, that you'll find different spellings in historical records, because clerks and census takers often misinterpreted different accents and dialects.

About the

_____

Family

Use photo corners or double-sided
tape to affix photo.

Mother: _____

Birth date and place: _____

Marriage date and place: _____

Death date and place: _____

Father: _____

Birth date and place: _____

Marriage date and place: _____

Death date and place: _____

Me: ....

Birth date and place: ....

Marriage date and place: ....

My Sibling: ....

Birth date and place: ....

Marriage date and place: ....

Spouse: ....

My Sibling: ....

Birth date and place: ....

Marriage date and place: ....

Spouse: ....

My Sibling: ....

Birth date and place: ....

Marriage date and place: ....

Spouse: ....

My Sibling: ....

Birth date and place: ....

Marriage date and place: ....

Spouse: ....

My Sibling: ....

Birth date and place: ....

Marriage date and place: ....

Spouse: ....

My Spouse:

Birth date and place:

My Child:

Birth date and place:

Marriage date and place:

Spouse:

My Child:

Birth date and place:

Marriage date and place:

Spouse:

My Child:

Birth date and place:

Marriage date and place:

Spouse:

My Child:

Birth date and place:

Marriage date and place:

Spouse:

My Child:

Birth date and place:

Marriage date and place:

Spouse:

My Grandchild: ....

Birth date and place: ....

Marriage date and place: ....

Spouse: ....

My Grandchild: ....

Birth date and place: ....

Marriage date and place: ....

Spouse: ....

My Grandchild: ....

Birth date and place: ....

Marriage date and place: ....

Spouse: ....

My Grandchild: ....

Birth date and place: ....

Marriage date and place: ....

Spouse: ....

My Grandchild: ....

Birth date and place: ....

Marriage date and place: ....

Spouse: ....

My Grandchild: ....

Birth date and place: ....

Marriage date and place: ....

Spouse: ....

About the

_____

Family

*Use photo corners or double-sided
tape to affix photo.*

Mother: ....

Birth date and place: ....

Marriage date and place: ....

Death date and place: ....

Father: ....

Birth date and place: ....

Marriage date and place: ....

Death date and place: ....

Me: ....

Birth date and place: ....

Marriage date and place: ....

My Sibling: ....

Birth date and place: ....

Marriage date and place: ....

Spouse: ....

My Sibling: ....

Birth date and place: ....

Marriage date and place: ....

Spouse: ....

My Sibling: ....

Birth date and place: ....

Marriage date and place: ....

Spouse: ....

My Sibling: ....

Birth date and place: ....

Marriage date and place: ....

Spouse: ....

My Sibling: ....

Birth date and place: ....

Marriage date and place: ....

Spouse: ....

My Spouse: ....

Birth date and place: ....

My Child: ....

Birth date and place: ....

Marriage date and place: ....

Spouse: ....

My Child: ....

Birth date and place: ....

Marriage date and place: ....

Spouse: ....

My Child: ....

Birth date and place: ....

Marriage date and place: ....

Spouse: ....

My Child: ....

Birth date and place: ....

Marriage date and place: ....

Spouse: ....

My Child: ....

Birth date and place: ....

Marriage date and place: ....

Spouse: ....

My Grandchild: ....

Birth date and place: ....

Marriage date and place: ....

Spouse: ....

My Grandchild: ....

Birth date and place: ....

Marriage date and place: ....

Spouse: ....

My Grandchild: ....

Birth date and place: ....

Marriage date and place: ....

Spouse: ....

My Grandchild: ....

Birth date and place: ....

Marriage date and place: ....

Spouse: ....

My Grandchild: ....

Birth date and place: ....

Marriage date and place: ....

Spouse: ....

My Grandchild: ....

Birth date and place: ....

Marriage date and place: ....

Spouse: ....

About the

....

Family

*Use photo corners or double-sided
tape to affix photo.*

Mother: ....

Birth date and place: ....

Marriage date and place: ....

Death date and place: ....

Father: ....

Birth date and place: ....

Marriage date and place: ....

Death date and place: ....

Me: ....

Birth date and place: ....

Marriage date and place: ....

My Sibling: ....

Birth date and place: ....

Marriage date and place: ....

Spouse: ....

My Sibling: ....

Birth date and place: ....

Marriage date and place: ....

Spouse: ....

My Sibling: ....

Birth date and place: ....

Marriage date and place: ....

Spouse: ....

My Sibling: ....

Birth date and place: ....

Marriage date and place: ....

Spouse: ....

My Sibling: ....

Birth date and place: ....

Marriage date and place: ....

Spouse: ....

My Spouse: ....

Birth date and place: ....

My Child: ....

Birth date and place: ....

Marriage date and place: ....

Spouse: ....

My Child: ....

Birth date and place: ....

Marriage date and place: ....

Spouse: ....

My Child: ....

Birth date and place: ....

Marriage date and place: ....

Spouse: ....

My Child: ....

Birth date and place: ....

Marriage date and place: ....

Spouse: ....

My Child: ....

Birth date and place: ....

Marriage date and place: ....

Spouse: ....

My Grandchild: ....

Birth date and place: ....

Marriage date and place: ....

Spouse: ....

My Grandchild: ....

Birth date and place: ....

Marriage date and place: ....

Spouse: ....

My Grandchild: ....

Birth date and place: ....

Marriage date and place: ....

Spouse: ....

My Grandchild: ....

Birth date and place: ....

Marriage date and place: ....

Spouse: ....

My Grandchild: ....

Birth date and place: ....

Marriage date and place: ....

Spouse: ....

My Grandchild: ....

Birth date and place: ....

Marriage date and place: ....

Spouse: ....

Family Name

Meaning: ....

Origin: ....

Stories about our name: ....

....

....

....

....

....

....

....

....

....

....

....

....

....

Source of information: ....

Family Name

Meaning: ....

Origin: ....

Stories about our name: ....

....

....

....

....

....

....

....

....

....

....

....

....

....

Source of information: ....

Family Name

Meaning: ....

Origin: ....

Stories about our name: ....

....

....

....

....

....

....

....

....

....

....

....

....

....

....

Source of information: ....

Family Name

Meaning: ....

Origin: ....

Stories about our name: ....

....

....

....

....

....

....

....

....

....

....

....

....

Source of information: ....

II

Our Family Tree

On the family information sheets in this chapter, you'll record details about each nuclear family, such as your maternal grandparents and their children (including your mom). You can also record this information on a five-generation ancestor chart.

It's OK if you end up with a lot of blank spaces because you don't know a name or date. You can leave the spaces as is and fill them in as you learn more from talking to relatives about family history (see the chapter three), or you can go looking for the missing details in basic genealogical records such as censuses and birth certificates.

The US government took censuses every ten years starting in 1790. Until 1850, censuses list the head of the household (usually the husband) and just the ages of other household members. In 1850 and later years, census takers recorded everyone's names, ages, relationships to the head of household, birthplaces, and other details. For privacy reasons, US census records are closed until 72 years after they're created. Virtually all of the 1890 census was ruined due to a fire.

You can search census records by name in online databases such as HeritageQuest Online and Ancestry Library Edition (both are available free through many public libraries), and through the subscrip-
tion service *<www.ancestry.com>* and for free at *<www.familysearch.org>*. You'll also find census records on microfilm at major public libraries, FamilySearch Family History Centers (find locations at *<www.familytreemagazine.com/fhcs>*), and US National Archives and Records Administration research facilities. Remember that spellings of names may have changed over the years, so look for variations, and don't discount a name that isn't spelled the way you think it should be.

Most states mandated vital record keeping in the late 1800s or early 1900s. Before that, towns and counties may have kept track of births, marriages, and deaths—even as early as the 1600s in some areas of New England. You can see state vital record-keeping dates on page 204 in the Reference Guide. How you get the records varies by place—you may need to order the certificate by mail from the state or county vital records office (fees range from $5 to $30) or view it on microfilm at a library or Family History Center. Look for instructions on the Web site for the vital records office in the state where your ancestor was born, married, or died (link to it from *<www.cdc.gov/nchs/w2w.htm>*).

About the

_____

Family

_Use photo corners or double-sided
tape to affix photo._

Husband: ....

Birth date and place: ....

Marriage date and place: ....

Death date and place: ....

Parents: ....

Wife: ....

Birth date and place: ....

Marriage date and place: ....

Death date and place: ....

Parents: ....

Child: ....

Birth date and place: ....

Marriage date and place: ....

Death date and place: ....

Child: ....

Birth date and place: ....

Marriage date and place: ....

Death date and place: ....

Child: ....

Birth date and place: ....

Marriage date and place: ....

Death date and place: ....

Child: ....

Birth date and place: ....

Marriage date and place: ....

Death date and place: ....

Child: ....

Birth date and place: ....

Marriage date and place: ....

Death date and place: ....

Other spouses for this couple: ....

Marriage date and place: ....

About the

_____

Family

*Use photo corners or double-sided
tape to affix photo.*

Husband: ....

Birth date and place: ....

Marriage date and place: ....

Death date and place: ....

Parents: ....

Wife: ....

Birth date and place: ....

Marriage date and place: ....

Death date and place: ....

Parents: ....

Child: ....

Birth date and place: ....

Marriage date and place: ....

Death date and place: ....

Child: ....

Birth date and place: ....

Marriage date and place: ....

Death date and place: ....

Child: ....

Birth date and place: ....

Marriage date and place: ....

Death date and place: ....

Child: ....

Birth date and place: ....

Marriage date and place: ....

Death date and place: ....

Child: ....

Birth date and place: ....

Marriage date and place: ....

Death date and place: ....

Other spouses for this couple: ....

Marriage date and place: ....

About the

_____

Family

*Use photo corners or double-sided
tape to affix photo.*

Husband: ....

Birth date and place: ....

Marriage date and place: ....

Death date and place: ....

Parents: ....

Wife: ....

Birth date and place: ....

Marriage date and place: ....

Death date and place: ....

Parents: ....

Child: ....

Birth date and place: ....

Marriage date and place: ....

Death date and place: ....

Child: ....

Birth date and place: ....

Marriage date and place: ....

Death date and place: ....

Child: ....

Birth date and place: ....

Marriage date and place: ....

Death date and place: ....

Child: ....

Birth date and place: ....

Marriage date and place: ....

Death date and place: ....

Child: ....

Birth date and place: ....

Marriage date and place: ....

Death date and place: ....

Other spouses for this couple: ....

Marriage date and place: ....

About the

Family

Use photo corners or double-sided
tape to affix photo.

Husband: ....

Birth date and place: ....

Marriage date and place: ....

Death date and place: ....

Parents: ....

Wife: ....

Birth date and place: ....

Marriage date and place: ....

Death date and place: ....

Parents: ....

Child: ....

Birth date and place: ....

Marriage date and place: ....

Death date and place: ....

Child: ....

Birth date and place: ....

Marriage date and place: ....

Death date and place: ....

Child: ....

Birth date and place: ....

Marriage date and place: ....

Death date and place: ....

Child: ....

Birth date and place: ....

Marriage date and place: ....

Death date and place: ....

Child: ....

Birth date and place: ....

Marriage date and place: ....

Death date and place: ....

Other spouses for this couple: ....

Marriage date and place: ....

About the

_____

Family

*Use photo corners or double-sided
tape to affix photo.*

Husband: ....

Birth date and place: ....

Marriage date and place: ....

Death date and place: ....

Parents: ....

Wife: ....

Birth date and place: ....

Marriage date and place: ....

Death date and place: ....

Parents: ....

Child: ....

Birth date and place: ....

Marriage date and place: ....

Death date and place: ....

Child: ....

Birth date and place: ....

Marriage date and place: ....

Death date and place: ....

Child: ....

Birth date and place: ....

Marriage date and place: ....

Death date and place: ....

Child: ....

Birth date and place: ....

Marriage date and place: ....

Death date and place: ....

Child: ....

Birth date and place: ....

Marriage date and place: ....

Death date and place: ....

Other spouses for this couple: ....

Marriage date and place: ....

About the

Family

*Use photo corners or double-sided
tape to affix photo.*

Husband: ....

Birth date and place: ....

Marriage date and place: ....

Death date and place: ....

Parents: ....

Wife: ....

Birth date and place: ....

Marriage date and place: ....

Death date and place: ....

Parents: ....

Child:

Birth date and place:

Marriage date and place:

Death date and place:

Child:

Birth date and place:

Marriage date and place:

Death date and place:

Child:

Birth date and place:

Marriage date and place:

Death date and place:

Child:

Birth date and place:

Marriage date and place:

Death date and place:

Child:

Birth date and place:

Marriage date and place:

Death date and place:

Other spouses for this couple:

Marriage date and place:

About the

Family

*Use photo corners or double-sided
tape to affix photo.*

Husband: ....

Birth date and place: ....

Marriage date and place: ....

Death date and place: ....

Parents: ....

Wife: ....

Birth date and place: ....

Marriage date and place: ....

Death date and place: ....

Parents: ....

Child: ....

Birth date and place: ....

Marriage date and place: ....

Death date and place: ....

Child: ....

Birth date and place: ....

Marriage date and place: ....

Death date and place: ....

Child: ....

Birth date and place: ....

Marriage date and place: ....

Death date and place: ....

Child: ....

Birth date and place: ....

Marriage date and place: ....

Death date and place: ....

Child: ....

Birth date and place: ....

Marriage date and place: ....

Death date and place: ....

Other spouses for this couple: ....

Marriage date and place: ....

About the

Family

*Use photo corners or double-sided
tape to affix photo.*

Husband: ....

Birth date and place: ....

Marriage date and place: ....

Death date and place: ....

Parents: ....

Wife: ....

Birth date and place: ....

Marriage date and place: ....

Death date and place: ....

Parents: ....

Child:

Birth date and place:

Marriage date and place:

Death date and place:

Child:

Birth date and place:

Marriage date and place:

Death date and place:

Child:

Birth date and place:

Marriage date and place:

Death date and place:

Child:

Birth date and place:

Marriage date and place:

Death date and place:

Child:

Birth date and place:

Marriage date and place:

Death date and place:

Other spouses for this couple:

Marriage date and place:

III

Memories & Traditions

Every family has an oral tradition of stories and legends the grown-ups tell the kids—how Great-Great-Grandpa saved money under his mattress for years to buy a ticket to America; how Uncle Fred proposed to Aunt Alice in a letter home from the European front during World War II. Families also hand down customs surrounding special occasions and holidays. This section has pages for saving information about your family's stories and traditions.

Interviewing family members is one of the first steps to gathering these traditions and discovering your family history. It's also the step people most often regret not taking after a beloved relative passes away. If you've lost older members of your family, talk to your brothers, sisters, and cousins—they may have heard family information you didn't. Consider interviewing family friends, too. Here's how to make those family history interviews successful.

1. Know your goals.
See the interview as a chance to spend time with a family member and let him (or her) talk about his life, rather than a chance to ask a lot of questions. The stories and information will follow from your shared conversation.

2. Set up the interview.
When you call to schedule your visit, say, "I'd like to find out more about our family history, and I was hoping you'd tell me some of the old stories." Ask if you can see your relative's old photos during the visit. If the relative doesn't know you well, it may help to bring along someone more familiar to him or her.

3. Focus on memories, not facts.

Your relative may become frustrated if you interrogate him about names and dates he doesn't remember. Instead, get him talking and insert name-and-date questions where appropriate. For example, when your grandfather's talking about how his parents met, ask, "What was your mom's maiden name?" or "When did they get married?"

4. Prepare a list of questions.

But use it as a guide, not a rigid framework. It's OK if the conversation leads to topics not on the list. See the box for suggested questions to ask.

5. Help your relative relax.

Sometimes a reticent relative will open up if you're doing an activity together, such as taking a walk, knitting, or fishing.

6. Use memory joggers.

Bring along old photos to spark memories about the people pictured. Bring your family tree chart, too. If possible, you can ask the family member you're interviewing to get out old heirlooms and photographs that you can look at together.

7. Record the conversation.

Jot down pertinent details during the interview, but writing too much is distracting. Instead, use a digital recorder or video camera. Test the equipment beforehand and bring extra batteries.

8. Just listen.

Everyone has his or her own view of what happened when. Keep in mind you may get inaccurate or partial information, so look for historical records to verify what relatives say. If you hear something you think isn't true, don't argue with the person—just make a note and keep the conversation moving.

9. Make a record.

When you get home, listen to your recording, look at your notes, and fill in an oral-history interview form. You can create a list of follow-up questions (if it's a relative you'll see again soon) or questions for other relatives based on the information from the interview.

10. Say thanks.

Don't forget to send a handwritten thank-you note. Then once you've gathered research and constructed more of your family's history, you can go back and share it with relatives that you interviewed. Everyone enjoys learning more about their ancestors, so the best way to say thanks to the relatives that you interview is to share what you learn along the way.

INTERVIEW QUESTIONS

- What did you do during the summer when you were a child?
- Did you have pets?
- What are your strongest memories of your siblings?
- What did you want to be when you grew up?
- How did you like school?
- What did you do on dates?
- How did you meet your husband/wife?
- What is the secret to a good relationship?
- What was your first job? What was your favorite job? Have you ever been fired or promoted?
- How are you like your parents? How are you different?
- What is the bravest thing you've ever done? The scariest? The dumbest?
- What was the hardest decision in your life?
- How did important historical events, like World War II, affect your family?
- What does it take to be a good parent?

Oral-History Interview

Use photo corners or double-sided tape to affix photo of interviewee.

Date and Place of birth: ....

Spouse: ....

Date and place of marriage: ....

Children's names (with dates and places of birth):

....

....

....

Childhood:

_____

_____

_____

_____

Growing up:

_____

_____

_____

_____

Jobs:

_____

_____

_____

_____

Settling down:

_____

_____

_____

_____

More memories:

_____

_____

_____

_____

_____

Oral-History Interview

Use photo corners or double-sided
tape to affix photo of interviewee.

Date and Place of birth: ....

Spouse: ....

Date and place of marriage: ....

Children's names (with dates and places of birth):

....

....

....

Childhood:

_____

_____

_____

_____

Growing up:

_____

_____

_____

_____

Jobs:

_____

_____

_____

_____

Settling down:

_____

_____

_____

_____

More memories:

_____

_____

_____

_____

Oral-History Interview

*Use photo corners or double-sided
tape to affix photo of interviewee.*

Date and Place of birth: ....

Spouse: ....

Date and place of marriage: ....

Children's names (with dates and places of birth):

....

....

....

....

Childhood:

....

....

....

....

Growing up:

....

....

....

....

Jobs:

....

....

....

....

Settling down:

....

....

....

....

More memories:

....

....

....

....

Oral-History Interview

Use photo corners or double-sided tape to affix photo of interviewee.

Date and Place of birth: ....

Spouse: ....

Date and place of marriage: ....

Children's names (with dates and places of birth):

....

....

....

....

Childhood:

....

....

....

....

Growing up:

....

....

....

....

Jobs:

....

....

....

....

Settling down:

....

....

....

....

More memories:

....

....

....

Family Traditions

Description of our tradition: ....

....

....

....

How it began: ....

....

....

....

When we observe it: ....

....

....

Favorite memories about this tradition: ....

....

....

....

....

....

Family Traditions

Description of our tradition: ....

....

....

....

How it began: ....

....

....

....

When we observe it: ....

....

....

Favorite memories about this tradition: ....

....

....

....

....

Family Traditions

Description of our tradition: ....

....

....

....

....

How it began: ....

....

....

....

....

When we observe it: ....

....

....

Favorite memories about this tradition: ....

....

....

....

....

....

Family Traditions

Description of our tradition: ....

....

....

....

....

How it began: ....

....

....

....

....

When we observe it: ....

....

....

Favorite memories about this tradition: ....

....

....

....

....

....

Family Stories

Title of story: ....

Who told this story: ....

Memories about this story: ....

....

....

....

....

....

....

....

....

....

....

....

....

Family Stories

Title of story: ....
....

Who told this story: ....
....

Memories about this story: ....
....
....
....
....
....
....
....
....
....
....
....
....

Family Stories

Title of story: ....

....

Who told this story: ....

....

Memories about this story: ....

....

....

....

....

....

....

....

....

....

....

....

Family Stories

Title of story: ....

Who told this story: ....

Memories about this story: ....

....

....

....

....

....

....

....

....

....

....

....

....

....

IV

Family Photographs

Your family photos are more than just pretty pictures, they're also visual connections with your ancestors, memory sparkers, and storehouses of clues about your family members' lives. They might even reveal where the family nose came from.

First, go through your albums and the shoe boxes stored in the basement and attic. Ask relatives if you can scan and print their photos, too (offer to share copies of your own pictures). Take out all the photos and sort them into families, with a separate pile for people you can't identify. Buy yourself a photo-labeling pencil (or get a soft-lead pencil) and, pressing lightly, label the back of each with names and the date and place the picture was taken. (See chapter eleven for a list of archival suppliers.) Scan your pictures and print copies of your favorites to frame and to put in this chapter of your keepsake book. Then fill in the blanks with as much information as you know about each one.

Finally, burn the images onto a CD or DVD. Your relatives may appreciate copies. Share paper or digital copies of the pictures from the mystery pile with your parents, grandparents, siblings, aunts, uncles, and cousins to see if anyone knows who's in them.

Put the original photos into archival storage: You can buy a photo-safe album and mount photos with photo corners (avoid glue and tape) or slip them into acid-free, lignin-free file folders. If you have a daguerreotype or tintype (a photo printed on metal, often contained in a wooden case), store it in an archival box. Keep photos in a living area of your home to maintain a stable temperature and humidity—avoid the attic or basement.

Now that you've preserved your treasured photos, take a closer look at them. What are the people wearing? How is their hair styled? What are their surroundings like? The answers can tell you when the photo was taken, what the occasion was, and whether your family was well off or of more modest means. Sometimes jewelry or other accessories in a photo reveal a person's religion, occupation, hobbies, or social clubs. Consult Maureen A. Taylor's *Family Photo Detective*, or her Photo Detective blog, *<http://blog.familytreemagazine.com/photodetectiveblog>*, to interpret clothing, hairstyles, accessories, and other details in photographs. Use a photo-identification worksheet to record your findings.

For unidentified pictures: Once you have an estimated date when each photo was taken, you can examine your family tree for families whose genders and ages match up with the people pictured. Through process of elimination, you may be able to put some names to the faces.

Photographic Record

*Use photo corners or double-sided
tape to affix photo.*

Date of photograph: ....

Place: ....

People pictured: ....

....

Occasion: ....

Owner of this picture: ....

Notes: ....

....

Photographic Record

*Use photo corners or double-sided
tape to affix photo.*

Date of photograph: ....

Place: ....

People pictured: ....

....

Occasion: ....

Owner of this picture: ....

Notes: ....

Photographic Record

Use photo corners or double-sided
tape to affix photo.

Date of photograph: ....

Place: ....

People pictured: ....

....

Occasion: ....

Owner of this picture: ....

Notes: ....

....

Photographic Record

*Use photo corners or double-sided
tape to affix photo.*

Date of photograph: ....

Place: ....

People pictured: ....

....

Occasion: ....

Owner of this picture: ....

Notes: ....

....

Photographic Record

*Use photo corners or double-sided
tape to affix photo.*

Date of photograph: ....

Place: ....

People pictured: ....

....

Occasion: ....

Owner of this picture: ....

Notes: ....

....

Photographic Record

*Use photo corners or double-sided
tape to affix photo.*

Date of photograph: ....

Place: ....

People pictured: ....

....

Occasion: ....

Owner of this picture: ....

Notes: ....

....

Photographic Record

Use photo corners or double-sided tape to affix photo.

Date of photograph: ....

Place: ....

People pictured: ....

....

Occasion: ....

Owner of this picture: ....

Notes: ....

....

Photographic Record

*Use photo corners or double-sided
tape to affix photo.*

Date of photograph: ....

Place: ....

People pictured: ....

....

Occasion: ....

Owner of this picture: ....

Notes: ....

....

Photographic Record

*Use photo corners or double-sided
tape to affix photo.*

Date of photograph: ....

Place: ....

People pictured: ....

....

Occasion: ....

Owner of this picture: ....

Notes: ....

....

Photographic Record

*Use photo corners or double-sided
tape to affix photo.*

Date of photograph: ....

Place: ....

People pictured: ....

....

Occasion: ....

Owner of this picture: ....

Notes: ....

....

Family Heirlooms

V

What makes something an heirloom? It's not the cost. Your precious heirlooms don't have to be worth money to be treasures—anything from Mom's diamond wedding band to the hankie Grandma embroidered can be a family heirloom. What matters is that it connects you with your family's legacy. In this section, you can keep track of your heirlooms' provenance (how they came to be in your family and how they were passed down) and the stories surrounding them. You also can include photographs and other information about them.

Of course your heirlooms have sentimental value. You'll also want to learn about certain items' monetary value for insurance purposes or to satisfy your curiosity. Examine pieces for markings and visit your library to find reference guides that can help you identify them. No luck? Consider having the item professionally appraised; look for appraisers, using the online directory at the National Association of Professional Appraisers' Web site, which is *<www. professionalappraisers.org>*.

Make sure these links with your past last for many generations to come by taking good care of them. Store any treasured or fragile item in a pest-free, darkened area with a steady, moderate temperature and humidity level—that rules out most attics and basements. Under your bed or in a closet in the living area of your home usually work well. Storage boxes and tissue papers should be acid- and lignin-free (purchase these materials from the archival suppliers listed in the Reference Guide). Find more advice on protecting family heirlooms in *How to Archive Family*

Keepsakes by Denise May Levenick. Here are more specific pointers for a variety of objects you may have inherited.

• **Jewelry:** If dirty, gently clean with a soft cloth and jewelry cleaner and then rinse and dry well before storing. See a jeweler for a more thorough cleaning if necessary. Keep pieces separated in velvet-lined containers so they don't scratch each other. Check hinges and clasps before wearing. Don't expose pieces to chlorine or steamy environments, and put on the piece after you apply hairspray and perfume.

• **Letters:** Remove letters from envelopes (save the envelopes), open pages flat, and get rid of any staples and paper clips. Place the pages in Mylar sleeves or archival file folders. Include a piece of buffered paper with 20th-century letters, which are likely written on acidic paper. Make copies for display or frequent handling and keep the original letters safely tucked away.

• **Newspaper clippings:** Place clippings in archival file folders or Mylar sleeves. Slip a sheet of buffered paper behind clippings that are on 20th-century newsprint, which is probably acidic. Photocopy clippings for handling and display.

• **Clothing and linens:** Loosely fold items in a muslin-lined box, padding creases, shoulders, and bodices with crumpled archival white tissue paper. Once a year, unfold and refold differently. Don't seal the box—fabrics need some air circulation. Remove dust with a vacuum-cleaner that has a stocking stretched over the nozzle. You can hand-wash most fabrics with a super-gentle detergent and lay flat to dry, but let a textile conservator clean fragile or heavily ornamented items.

• **Books:** If the book is fragile, tie bookbinder's will tape around it to secure the covers and keep it in a book box sized to fit. Otherwise, store the book on a shelf with similar-sized tomes and dust occasionally with a soft brush. Avoid pulling on the spine to remove it. Don't use staples or tape on a book; repairs are best left to professional archivists (find a referral service on the Academy of Certified Archivists' Web site, *<www.certifiedarchivists.org>*).

• **China and glassware:** You can purchase padded or cardboard storage containers especially for dishes. Use padding between stacked plates and bowls. In your cupboard, store cups and glasses on their bases rather than on the fragile rims. Gently dust china on display with a soft brush, being especially careful around painted gilded trim, which can flake off. Handwashing the dishes in mild detergent is best (pad the sink with a dish towel to prevent breakage).

• **Silver:** Polish with nonabrasive silver polish and a soft cloth (use a cotton swab in intricate areas). To help prevent tarnish, avoid contact with eggs, onions, peas, rubber, and latex. Salt is corrosive, too, so empty silver saltshakers after use. Nix dishwashing in favor of handwashing; dry right away. Store in polyethylene bags or wrap in cotton flannel, and keep in a low-humidity environment.

• **Wood furniture:** When arranging furniture, place antique items away from direct sunlight. A steady humidity level will help keep the wood from expanding and contracting. Instead of polish, which can build up, apply a thin layer of furniture paste wax once a year. Dust regularly with a slightly damp, soft cloth.

Heirloom Recording Form

*Use photo corners or double-sided
tape to affix photo.*

Description: ....

Provenance: ....

Memories about this heirloom: ....

....

....

....

....

Notes: ....

....

Heirloom Recording Form

Use photo corners or double-sided tape to affix photo.

Description: ....

Provenance: ....

Memories about this heirloom: ....

....

....

....

....

Notes: ....

....

Heirloom Recording Form

*Use photo corners or double-sided
tape to affix photo.*

Description: ....

Provenance: ....

Memories about this heirloom: ....

....

....

....

....

Notes: ....

....

Heirloom Recording Form

Use photo corners or double-sided tape to affix photo.

Description: ....

Provenance: ....

Memories about this heirloom: ....

....

....

....

....

Notes: ....

....

Heirloom Recording Form

*Use photo corners or double-sided
tape to affix photo.*

Description: ....

Provenance: ....

Memories about this heirloom: ....

....

....

....

....

Notes: ....

....

Heirloom
Recording Form

*Use photo corners or double-sided
tape to affix photo.*

Description: ....

Provenance: ....

Memories about this heirloom: ....

....

....

....

....

Notes: ....

....

VI
Relatives in the Service

Chances are someone in your family's history served the in the military, whether domestically or abroad. Meanwhile, those who stayed behind contributed to the war effort by going to work in factories, volunteering for soldiers' aid organizations, growing gardens, conserving fuel, caring for widows and orphans, and gathering care packages for soldiers. You can honor this legacy by learning more about your relatives' military service and documenting it for future generations to remember.

Service records (for enrollment and discharge, honors and awards, rank, battles participated in, and more) before World War I are at the US National Archives and Records Administration (NARA) in Washington, DC. Records of pensions that injured soldiers or surviving widows and children could file for are also located in the NARA. If you know the person's full name, birthplace, and approximate dates of service, you can order copies of his records, using NARA's online ordering system. Learn more about requesting these military records at *<archives.gov/ veterans/military-service-records/pre-ww-1-records.html#nwctb-list>*.

Service records for those who served in World War I and later are in NARA's National Personnel Records Center in St. Louis, MO. Unfortunately, records of many 20th-century Army and Air Force personnel were lost in a fire. Some surviving records may be limited to next-of-kin for privacy reasons. The best way to find out if records for your family member are available is to request a search for your relative's records following the instructions online at *<http:// archives.gov/st-louis/military-personnel/standard-form-180.html>*.

Some military records and databases of information taken from records are part of subscription sites including Ancestry.com and Fold3.com *<www.fold3.com>* and the free FamilySearch Records Search *<www. familysearch.org>*.

Military Service Record

*Use photo corners or double-sided
tape to affix photo.*

Name:

Birth date and place:

Parents:

Marriage date and place:

Spouse:

Death date and place:

Burial place:

Branch of service:

Service dates:

Rank and unit:

Conflicts served in:

Battles:

Awards and decorations:

Wartime memories:

Military Service Record

*Use photo corners or double-sided
tape to affix photo.*

Name: ....

Birth date and place: ....

Parents: ....

Marriage date and place: ....

Spouse: ....

Death date and place: ....

Burial place: ....

Branch of service: ....

Service dates:

Rank and unit:

Conflicts served in:

Battles:

Awards and decorations:

Wartime memories:

Military Service Record

*Use photo corners or double-sided
tape to affix photo.*

Name: ....

Birth date and place: ....

Parents: ....

Marriage date and place: ....

Spouse: ....

Death date and place: ....

Burial place: ....

Branch of service: ....

Service dates:

Rank and unit:

Conflicts served in:

Battles:

Awards and decorations:

Wartime memories:

Military Service Record

*Use photo corners or double-sided
tape to affix photo.*

Name: ....

Birth date and place: ....

Parents: ....

Marriage date and place: ....

Spouse: ....

Death date and place: ....

Burial place: ....

Branch of service: ....

Service dates:

Rank and unit:

Conflicts served in:

Battles:

Awards and decorations:

Wartime memories:

Military Service Record

Use photo corners or double-sided tape to affix photo.

Name:

Birth date and place:

Parents:

Marriage date and place:

Spouse:

Death date and place:

Burial place:

Branch of service:

Service dates:

Rank and unit:

Conflicts served in:

Battles:

Awards and decorations:

Wartime memories:

Military Service Record

*Use photo corners or double-sided
tape to affix photo.*

Name:

Birth date and place:

Parents:

Marriage date and place:

Spouse:

Death date and place:

Burial place:

Branch of service:

Service dates:

Rank and unit:

Conflicts served in:

Battles:

Awards and decorations:

Wartime memories:

Military Service Record

Use photo corners or double-sided tape to affix photo.

Name: ....

Birth date and place: ....

Parents: ....

Marriage date and place: ....

Spouse: ....

Death date and place: ....

Burial place: ....

Branch of service: ....

Service dates: ....

....

....

Rank and unit: ....

....

Conflicts served in: ....

....

....

....

Battles: ....

....

....

Awards and decorations: ....

....

....

....

Wartime memories: ....

....

....

....

....

....

VII

Relatives Making News

People don't have to be famous to be in the newspaper. Birth and marriage announcements, obituaries, graduation notices and society reports of comings and goings all mention ordinary folks. Services such as NewsBank *<www.newsbank.com>* (available free through public libraries) and GenealogyBank *<www. genealogybank.com>* (by subscription) let you search digitized articles from hundreds of newspapers. Most small-town newspapers are available only on microfilm—usually at public libraries located near the area where the newspaper was published. You can find out what papers your ancestors likely read on the Library of Congress' Chronicling America Web site, *<chroniclingamerica.loc.gov>*.

Your ancestors also may be mentioned in a history book about the place they lived. Or a distant cousin you've never met might have written a book about your family members. Local libraries located where your ancestors lived are most likely to have this kind of book. If that's too far away, search the catalog online and see if your library can borrow it for you through interlibrary loan. But you also may find such books online in local history collections offered by HeritageQuest Online (an online service available free through many public libraries) or *<www.ancestry. com>*.

Most every student made an appearance in his or her yearbooks. Not only will you see a photo of your relative as a teen or young adult, you'll learn all about his activities and interests. Look for high school and college yearbooks at libraries and the Web sites mentioned above. A local public library—or the school library—probably has old editions.

In the News

*Use photo corners or double-sided
tape to affix press clipping.*

Name: ....

Publication title, author, date, and page number: ....

....

Description of coverage: ....

....

Notes: ....

....

....

....

In the News

*Use photo corners or double-sided
tape to affix press clipping*

Name: ....

Publication title, author, date, and page number: ....

....

....

Description of coverage: ....

....

....

Notes: ....

....

....

....

....

In the News

*Use photo corners or double-sided
tape to affix press clipping*

Name: ....

Publication title, author, date, and page number: ....

....

....

Description of coverage: ....

....

....

Notes: ....

....

....

....

....

In the News

*Use photo corners or double-sided
tape to affix press clipping.*

Name: ....

Publication title, author, date, and page number: ....

....

....

Description of coverage: ....

....

....

Notes: ....

....

....

....

In the News

*Use photo corners or double-sided
tape to affix press clipping.*

Name: ....

Publication title, author, date, and page number: ....
....
....

Description of coverage: ....
....
....

Notes: ....
....
....
....
....

In the News

*Use photo corners or double-sided
tape to affix press clipping*

Name: ....

Publication title, author, date, and page number: ....

....

....

Description of coverage: ....

....

....

Notes: ....

....

....

....

In the News

*Use photo corners or double-sided
tape to affix press clipping*

Name: ....

Publication title, author, date, and page number: ....

....

....

Description of coverage: ....

....

....

Notes: ....

....

....

....

....

In the News

*Use photo corners or double-sided
tape to affix press clipping*

Name: ....

Publication title, author, date, and page number: ....

....

....

Description of coverage: ....

....

....

Notes: ....

....

....

....

....

In the News

*Use photo corners or double-sided
tape to affix press clipping.*

Name: ....

Publication title, author, date, and page number: ....

....

....

Description of coverage: ....

....

....

Notes: ....

....

....

....

In the News

*Use photo corners or double-sided
tape to affix press clipping.*

Name: ....

Publication title, author, date, and page number: ....

....

....

Description of coverage: ....

....

....

Notes: ....

....

....

....

VIII

Places

Remember Christmases at Grandma and Grandpa's house? How about the scent of honeysuckle mingling with the sounds of crickets and laughter during summer parties at Aunt Helen's? Dad's retelling of his immigrant grandparents' stories about life back in the old country?

Family memories and stories revolve around places just as much as they do people. But as relatives scatter over time, and modern families become more and more spread out, that geographic legacy is easily lost. In this section, you'll find pages to create a record of where your family is now and where you've been—including places here and abroad.

If you've lost track of some old family homesteads, it isn't difficult to learn where relatives lived in the past. Begin by locating your kin in censuses (described in chapter two) and city directories—yesterday's equivalent of modern-day phone books—available through genealogical libraries. These will often yield an address, which you can use to chase down deeds or land records.

If your family settled early in a state other than the original US colonies and a few others (public-land states), you can likely find the patent recording their purchase of land at the Bureau of Land Management General Land Office Records Web site, *<www.glorecords.blm.gov>*. After you've found a homestead, it's also worth checking with local historical societies to see if they have photos or documents relating to your family's residences.

You probably have some sort of lore surrounding your family's foreign origins—the story might go something like, "We're Scotch-Irish," or "Great-Grandma came from Hungary." At some point, you may want to know the specifics and perhaps even trace your family back in the old country.

Retracing your ancestors' journey starts with your relatives today. Someone might've heard the tale of Great-Grandma's journey to America or have documents detailing where she came from. See chapter three for hints on interviewing relatives, and look for these helpful items.

Perhaps someone has saved letters or postcards exchanged between Great-Grandma and her relatives back home. During times of duress, relatives may have corresponded to ask for help—for example, during World War II European relatives may have reached out to their American cousins for aid. Or maybe Uncle Alan still has Great-Uncle John's answer to a request for genealogy information.

Obituaries often reference where an immigrant came from, sometimes vaguely ("He came to this country from Italy in 1874"), but other times by naming a specific city or village. And because of the pride associated with becoming a citizen, many families often saved members' naturalization papers. Immigrants to the United States must live in the country for three to five years before applying for citizenship, so naturalization applications usually list details such as the town the applicant came from and the citizenship he or she renounced in swearing allegiance to a new nation.

If relatives don't have obituaries and naturalization papers, you can get them through other means. Newspapers are widely available on microfilm and online (chapter seven tells you where to look). For naturalization papers, first check online at *<www.fold3.com>*. Next, try the Family History Library in Salt Lake City (listed in the Reference Guide), which has many microfilmed naturalization records you can rent through one of its local Family History Centers. Keep in mind naturalizations until 1906 could file for citizenship in any court—they could even start the process in one court and finish in another. For naturalizations in 1906

and later, you can file a Freedom of Information Act request with US Citizenship and Immigration Services, using form G-639 (see the Web site *<www.uscis.gov/genealogy>*). It's a slow process, though, so make it your path of last resort.

Once you've identified who immigrated, you can look for a passenger list documenting his or her journey to America. The United States began requiring ships to submit passenger manifests in 1820, and these records become more detailed over time. One key fact to keep in mind: The records were filled out by people at the port of departure, not by immigration officials in America. That means you'll need to look for your ancestor under the name he used in the old country. (It also means that families' names weren't changed at Ellis Island—a common misconception.)

The US National Archives and Records Administration has kept passenger lists of all US ports, including New York, Boston, Philadelphia, New Orleans, Galveston, San Francisco, and other coastal cities. You can find microfilmed versions at genealogical libraries (see a list in the Reference Guide) and National Archives research facilities. Or you can search for them online at *<www.ancestry.com>* (subscription required) or a library offering Ancestry Library Edition. Other good resources to check are immigrant indexes available in many libraries, such as the Passenger and Immigration Lists Index and Germans to America series.

As the country's largest immigration hub, New York City has several special online resources: Ellis Island's Web site, *<www.ellisisland.org>*, has a searchable database of the 17-million-plus immigrants who arrived there between 1892 and 1924. You can even see images of the ships' manifests on the Web site. Ellis Island's predecessor, Castle Garden—the country's first immigration station—also has a searchable database of arriving passengers at *<castlegarden.org>*. To see the passenger lists, however, you'll have to look them up on microfilm or on *<www.ancestry.com>*.

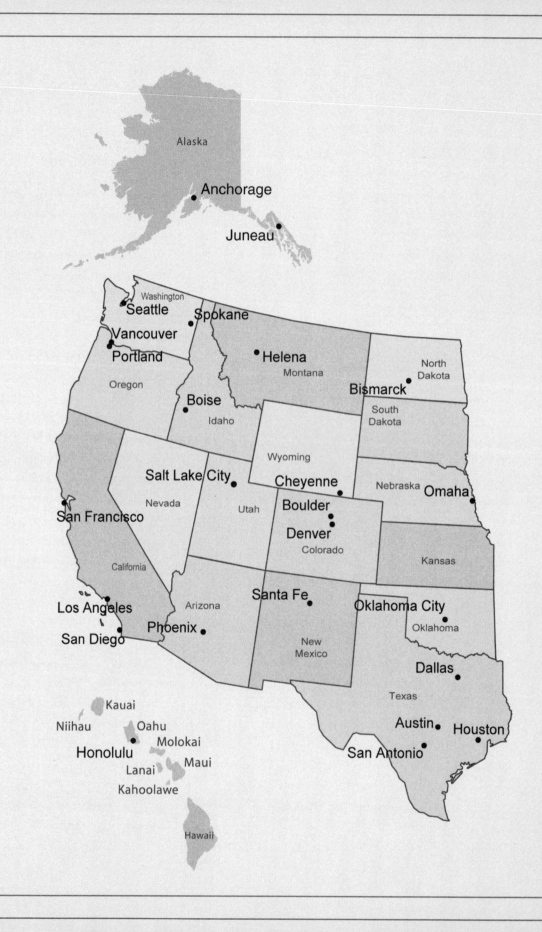

Alaska

Anchorage

Juneau

Washington
Seattle
Spokane
Vancouver
Helena
Portland
Montana
Bismarck
North
Dakota
Oregon
Boise
South
Dakota
Idaho

Wyoming

Salt Lake City
Cheyenne
Nebraska
Omaha

Nevada
Boulder
Utah
San Francisco
Denver
Colorado
Kansas

California
Santa Fe
Oklahoma City

Los Angeles
Arizona
Oklahoma
Phoenix
San Diego
New
Mexico

Dallas

Kauai
Texas
Niihau
Oahu
Austin
Houston
Molokai
Honolulu
Maui
San Antonio
Lanai
Kahoolawe

Hawaii

The United States

On this map, mark locations your family has lived, today or in the past.

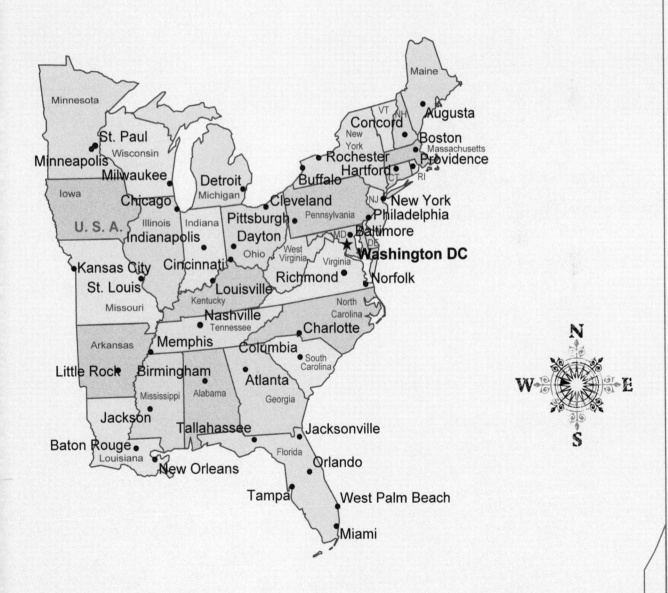

Family or Family Branch   **Hometown**

Family or Family Branch   **Hometown**

Family or Family Branch	Hometown

Family or Family Branch   **Hometown**

Family or Family Branch **Hometown**

Family or Family Branch

Hometown

Photos of Family Home

*Use photo corners or double-sided
tape to affix photo.*

Family Home

Location/address: ....

....

Relatives living there: ....

....

....

....

Dates owned or occupied: ....

Description of the home: ....

....

....

Family milestones that took place there: ....

....

....

Special memories of this home: ....

....

....

Photos of Family Home

*Use photo corners or double-sided
tape to affix photo.*

Family Home

Location/address: ....

....

Relatives living there: ....

....

....

....

Dates owned or occupied: ....

....

Description of the home: ....

....

....

Family milestones that took place there: ....

....

....

....

Special memories of this home: ....

....

....

....

Photos of Family Home

Use photo corners or double-sided tape to affix photo.

Family Home

Location/address: ....

....

Relatives living there: ....

....

....

....

Dates owned or occupied: ....

....

Description of the home: ....

....

....

Family milestones that took place there: ....

....

....

Special memories of this home: ....

....

....

....

Photos of Family Home

*Use photo corners or double-sided
tape to affix photo.*

Family Home

Location/address: ....

Relatives living there: ....

....

....

....

Dates owned or occupied: ....

....

Description of the home: ....

....

....

Family milestones that took place there: ....

....

....

Special memories of this home: ....

....

....

....

Photos of Family Home

Use photo corners or double-sided tape to affix photo.

Family Home

Location/address: ....

Relatives living there: ....

....

....

Dates owned or occupied: ....

Description of the home: ....

....

Family milestones that took place there: ....

....

....

Special memories of this home: ....

....

....

Photos of Family Home

Use photo corners or double-sided tape to affix photo.

Family Home

Location/address: ....

....

Relatives living there: ....

....

....

....

Dates owned or occupied: ....

....

Description of the home: ....

....

....

Family milestones that took place there: ....

....

....

....

Special memories of this home: ....

....

....

....

Photos of Family Home

Use photo corners or double-sided tape to affix photo.

Family Home

Location/address:

Relatives living there:

Dates owned or occupied:

Description of the home:

Family milestones that took place there:

Special memories of this home:

Photos of Family Home

*Use photo corners or double-sided
tape to affix photo.*

Family Home

Location/address:

Relatives living there:

Dates owned or occupied:

Description of the home:

Family milestones that took place there:

Special memories of this home:

Family Recipes

IX

When it comes to family, the way to our hearts truly is through our stomachs. Who doesn't fondly associate certain relatives with favorite foods shared around the family table? Mom's fried chicken. Uncle Tony's spaghetti sauce. Grandma's peanut butter cookies.

Those beloved dishes are a legacy worth passing on. Here are steps you can take to ensure that future generations will be able to savor your family's food history. Find more advice for collection family recipes in *From the Family Kitchen* by Gena Philibert-Ortega.

1. Note favorite foods.

Begin by making a list of the dishes traditionally served at your family's table on Christmas, Thanksgiving, Passover, the Fourth of July, or whichever holidays you celebrate. Note who usually makes each dish, how it's served, and what characteristics make it special or unique.

2. Approach the chefs behind each dish and ask them to share their recipes.

You may encounter relatives who follow the "pinch of this, dash of that" method of cooking—rather than precisely measuring ingredients, they add by feel and by memory. In these cases, see if you (or another relative) can observe the cook in action so you can measure each ingredient and record each step as it happens. Don't forget to also ask how their creations came to be family traditions.

3. Talk to the eldest members of your family to learn about past generations' food traditions.

What did their parents and grandparents serve at their dinner tables? Which dishes were staples at holiday gatherings? If those recipes have been lost, search for equivalents online and in cookbooks, especially period volumes such as Fannie Farmer's *Boston Cooking-School Cook Book* (the 1918 edition is online at *<www.bartleby.com/87>*).

4. Gather ethnic recipes.

Some of your family's favorites might reflect your ethnic heritage—strudel, sopapillas, spanakopita. Try expanding that repertoire to other foods your ancestors ate. It's easy to learn about traditional ethnic cuisine: Search the Web for phrases such as Swedish recipes or traditional Indian dishes to turn up recipe sites or browse your favorite bookstore's shelves for international cookbooks.

5. Create a culinary record.

This section contains Recipe History Recorder pages to help you preserve the heritage and history behind your family's food traditions, as well as the recipes themselves. You'll also find recipe cards to fill out and share with relatives or keep in your kitchen for everyday use.

Helpful Abbreviations

bu	bushel
c	cup
fl	fluid
hr	hours
gal	gallon
lb	pound
min	minutes
oz	ounce
pkg	package
pk	peck
pt.	pint
qt	quart
t, tsp	teaspoon
T, tbs	tablespoon

Cooking Temperatures

slow oven	300 degrees Fahrenheit
moderate oven	350 degrees
quick oven	375 to 400 degrees
hot oven	400 to 425 degrees

Equivalents and Measurements

dash	¼ teaspoon or less
saltspoon	¼ teaspoon
pinch	⅛ teaspoon or less
1 dram	¾ teaspoon
kitchen spoon	1 teaspoon
1 tablespoon	3 teaspoons
1 fluid ounce	2 tablespoons or 16 dram
1 jigger	1½ fluid ounces
wineglass	¼ cup
½ cup	8 tablespoons
1 gill	½ cup
1 cup	8 fluid ounces
teacup	scant ¾ cup
coffeecup	scant cup
tumbler	1 cup
1 pound	16 ounces
1 pint	2 cups
1 quart	4 cups
1 pottle	2 quarts
1 gallon	4 quarts or 16 cups
1 peck	2 gallons or 8 quarts
1 bushel	4 peck

Recipe History Recorder

Dish: ....

Who made it: ....

When it was served: ....

History and memories of this dish:

....

....

....

....

....

....

....

....

....

....

....

Ingredients: ....

....

....

....

....

Instructions: ....

....

....

....

Hints: ....

....

....

*Use photo corners or double-sided
tape to affix photo.*

Recipe History Recorder

Dish: ....

Who made it: ....

When it was served: ....

History and memories of this dish:

....

....

....

....

....

....

....

....

....

....

Ingredients:

....

....

....

....

Instructions:

....

....

....

....

Hints:

....

....

*Use photo corners or double-sided
tape to affix photo.*

Recipe History Recorder

Dish: ....

Who made it: ....

When it was served: ....

History and memories of this dish:

....

....

....

....

....

....

....

....

....

....

Ingredients:

Instructions:

Hints:

*Use photo corners or double-sided
tape to affix photo.*

Recipe History Recorder

Dish: ....

Who made it: ....

When it was served: ....

History and memories of this dish:

....

....

....

....

....

....

....

....

....

....

....

Ingredients:

....

....

....

....

Instructions:

....

....

....

....

Hints:

....

....

....

*Use photo corners or double-sided
tape to affix photo.*

Recipe History Recorder

Dish: ....

Who made it: ....

When it was served: ....

History and memories of this dish: ....

....

....

....

....

....

....

....

....

....

....

....

Ingredients:

....

....

....

....

Instructions:

....

....

....

....

Hints:

....

....

*Use photo corners or double-sided
tape to affix photo.*

Recipe History Recorder

Dish: ....

Who made it: ....

When it was served: ....

History and memories of this dish:

....

....

....

....

....

....

....

....

....

....

Ingredients:

....

....

....

....

....

Instructions:

....

....

....

....

Hints:

....

....

*Use photo corners or double-sided
tape to affix photo.*

Recipe

From the kitchen of: ....

Makes .... servings

Ingredients: ....

....

....

....

....

....

....

....

Instructions: ....

....

....

....

....

....

....

....

....

....

Recipe

From the kitchen of: ....

Makes .... servings

Ingredients: ....

....

....

....

....

....

....

....

Instructions: ....

....

....

....

....

....

....

....

....

Recipe

From the kitchen of: ....

Makes .... servings

Ingredients: ....

....

....

....

....

....

....

....

Instructions: ....

....

....

....

....

....

....

....

....

Recipe

From the kitchen of: ....

Makes .... servings

Ingredients: ....

....

....

....

....

....

....

....

Instructions: ....

....

....

....

....

....

....

....

....

....

....

....

Recipe

From the kitchen of: ....

Makes .... servings

Ingredients: ....

....

....

....

....

....

....

....

Instructions: ....

....

....

....

....

....

....

....

....

....

....

Recipe

From the kitchen of: ....

Makes .... servings

Ingredients: ....

....

....

....

....

....

....

....

Instructions: ....

....

....

....

....

....

....

....

....

Recipe

From the kitchen of: ....

Makes .... servings

Ingredients: ....

....

....

....

....

....

....

....

Instructions: ....

....

....

....

....

....

....

....

....

Recipe

From the kitchen of: ....

Makes .... servings

Ingredients: ....

....

....

....

....

....

....

....

Instructions: ....

....

....

....

....

....

....

....

Recipe

From the kitchen of: ....

Makes .... servings

Ingredients: ....

....

....

....

....

....

....

....

Instructions: ....

....

....

....

....

....

....

....

....

Recipe

From the kitchen of: ....

Makes .... servings

Ingredients: ....

....

....

....

....

....

....

Instructions: ....

....

....

....

....

....

....

....

....

....

....

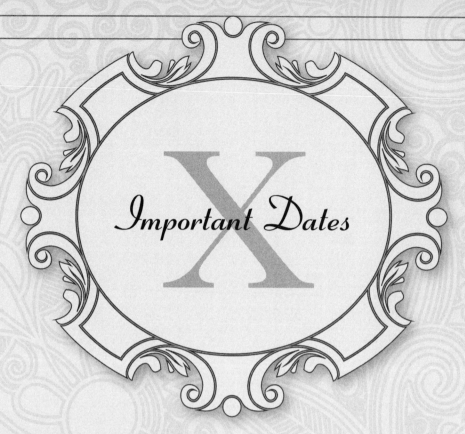

X

Important Dates

Birthdays, anniversaries, holidays, weddings, graduations—families have a lot of dates to keep track of. Toss extended family into the mix, and the timeline gets even tougher to keep straight.

The calendar in this section is designed as a central place to record all of your clan's important dates. You'll notice it's a perpetual calendar—without a specific year or days of the week—so it never goes out of date.

For each day of the month, there's space to record key events. If you expand your chronology to include ancestral generations, your calendar also becomes a snapshot of your family history. Some good milestones to record:

- **Birthdays:** Write the person's name and year he or she was born. Don't limit this to living relatives—add any ancestral birth dates you know. For more-distant relations, you may want to include a parenthetical reminder of their place in the family tree, such as "Gerry Morris' mother" or "Rita's brother."
- **Anniversaries:** Fill in the couple's names, including the wife's maiden name, and year of the marriage.
- **Deaths:** Note when beloved relatives and ancestors passed away. Again, you might choose to note relation-ships, and consider including the cemetery name and burial date if you know it.
- **Military service:** Depending on your relatives' service records (see chapter six for help finding these), you could include a number of red-letter moments—enlist-ment or discharge, battles or other actions, and awards or honors. For example: "Grandpa fought in Battle of Iwo Jima, Pacific Theater, World War II, 1945."
- **Immigration/migration:** Write the date your an-cestor arrived in America, noting the port of entry, ship's name, and any other interesting details. You may want to record other major relocations, too: "Grandma moved from Indiana to Arizona, 2002" or "Jeremiah Norton purchased 1,100 acres in Iowa, 1894."
- **Naturalization:** Record the date your immigrant ancestor attained citizenship.

Once you've filled in all these milestones, make copies to share with your relatives so everyone can stay up to date. And with all that family history at your fingertips, you may even decide to plan your next reunion or get-together around a fun or meaningful family event.

Family Holidays

Record the names and dates of the holidays your family celebrates here. Include
the national, religious, and other traditional holidays that you currently celebrate
and those that your ancestors celebrated.

Holiday	Date Observed

January

1

2

3

4

5

6

7

8

9

10

11

12

13

14

15

16

17

18

19

20

21

22

23

24

25

26

27

28

29

30

31

February

1

2

3

4

5

6

7

8

9

10

11

12

13

14

15

16

17

18

19

20

21

22

23

24

25

26

27

28

29

March

1 .... 2 ....

....

....

3 .... 4 ....

....

....

5 .... 6 ....

....

....

7 .... 8 ....

....

....

9 .... 10 ....

....

....

11 .... 12 ....

....

....

13 .... 14 ....

....

....

15 ....

....

....

16 .... 17 ....

....

18 .... 19 ....

....

20 .... 21 ....

....

22 .... 23 ....

....

24 .... 25 ....

....

26 .... 27 ....

....

28 .... 29 ....

....

30 .... 31 ....

....

....

April

1

2

3

4

5

6

7

8

9

10

11

12

13

14

15

16

17

18

19

20

21

22

23

24

25

26

27

28

29

30

May

1 .... 2 ....

....

3 .... 4 ....

....

5 .... 6 ....

....

7 .... 8 ....

....

9 .... 10 ....

....

11 .... 12 ....

....

13 .... 14 ....

....

15 ....

....

16 .... 17 ....

18 .... 19 ....

20 .... 21 ....

22 .... 23 ....

24 .... 25 ....

26 .... 27 ....

28 .... 29 ....

30 .... 31 ....

June

1

2

3

4

5

6

7

8

9

10

11

12

13

14

15

16

17

18

19

20

21

22

23

24

25

26

27

28

29

30

July

1 .... 2 ....

3 .... 4 ....

5 .... 6 ....

7 .... 8 ....

9 .... 10 ....

11 .... 12 ....

13 .... 14 ....

15 ....

16

17

18

19

20

21

22

23

24

25

26

27

28

29

30

31

August

1

2

3

4

5

6

7

8

9

10

11

12

13

14

15

16

17

18

19

20

21

22

23

24

25

26

27

28

29

30

31

September

1 .... 2 ....

3 .... 4 ....

5 .... 6 ....

7 .... 8 ....

9 .... 10 ....

11 .... 12 ....

13 .... 14 ....

15 ....

16 ....

17 ....

....

....

18 ....

19 ....

....

....

20 ....

21 ....

....

....

22 ....

23 ....

....

....

24 ....

25 ....

....

....

26 ....

27 ....

....

....

28 ....

29 ....

....

....

30 ....

....

....

October

1

2

3

4

5

6

7

8

9

10

11

12

13

14

15

16 .... 17 ....

....

18 .... 19 ....

....

20 .... 21 ....

....

22 .... 23 ....

....

24 .... 25 ....

....

26 .... 27 ....

....

28 .... 29 ....

....

30 .... 31 ....

....

....

November

1

2

3

4

5

6

7

8

9

10

11

12

13

14

15

16

17

18

19

20

21

22

23

24

25

26

27

28

29

30

December

1 .... 2 ....

....

3 .... 4 ....

....

5 .... 6 ....

....

7 .... 8 ....

....

9 .... 10 ....

....

11 .... 12 ....

....

13 .... 14 ....

....

15 ....

....

16 .... 17 ....

....

....

18 .... 19 ....

....

....

20 .... 21 ....

....

....

22 .... 23 ....

....

....

24 .... 25 ....

....

....

26 .... 27 ....

....

....

28 .... 29 ....

....

....

30 .... 31 ....

....

....

XI

Reference Guide

So you've decided you want to dive deeper into your family history. Congratulations! You're about to embark on a fun and rewarding journey. This section contains a wealth of tools and tips to start your search on the right foot. You'll also find resources related to the topics covered within earlier chapters of this book.

RULES OF THUMB FOR ROOTS RESEARCHERS

1. Always work backward from present to past.
Resist the temptation to skip generations—you might end up tracing the wrong ancestors.

2. Take family legends with a grain of salt.
Memories fade, and stories often change as they're passed from person to person (remember playing "Telephone" as a kid?). Just because Grandma said so doesn't make it true. Be aware that family stories may be unintentionally (and, yes, sometimes intentionally) changed or embellished, and be open to other possibilities.

3. Go beyond the Web.
Although you can make a lot of progress online, don't expect to find everything about your family history on the Internet. Plenty of records and information are still available only on microfilm or paper, requiring a trip to a library or archive (on the bright side, you can usually identify those records and plan your outing online).

4. Focus on one family at a time.
Once you start racking up ancestors and distant cousins on your family tree, it gets tough to keep all those names and dates straight. Pick one group or family line to research at a time so you don't get mixed up.

5. Forget the "right" spellings.
Don't assume a person is your relative because his last name is spelled the same as yours or, conversely, rule out a potential ancestor because his name is spelled "wrong." People weren't so finicky about spelling in the past. As a result, your ancestors' names will be spelled different

ways. Look for variations in indexes and databases.

6. Confirm identities.

You might take for granted that a person with the right name in the right location has to be your ancestor. Not necessarily—especially if it's a common name. Use other identifying information, such as age and spouse's name, to make sure you've got the right William Smith.

7. Think like a detective.

Solving the mystery of your family's past is what makes genealogy fun. Check every source, ferret out every clue, and don't be afraid to ask others for help.

CREATE A KEEPSAKE FAMILY HISTORY CD

A slide show of digital photos and old documents is a great way to share family history—and back up those memories in case disaster strikes. All you'll need to create your own keepsake is blank CD-Rs, labels, and cases; a computer with a CD burner; Your electronic photos and records; and PowerPoint or another slide show software program. (These instructions work on Windows and Macintosh computers.)

1. Choose the images and documents you want in your slide show, copy the files, and put them all in one folder. As a guideline for how much you can include, CDs generally hold 650 to 700MB of data—about 325 2MB pictures.

2. Determine the order in which you want your files to appear and rename them so they display in that order. This will make it easier to place your photos in the slide show.

3. Open PowerPoint and create a new presentation. Use your first slide as a title page—like "Robinson Family History, 1811–2009."

4. On the next slide, add your first photo or document. Go to Insert>Picture>From File, locate the folder where you saved your files, and select the first one, and then click OK.

5. Add an explanatory caption beneath the image.

6. Continue adding one photo or document per slide,

including a caption with each, and saving your work as you go.

7. Next exit PowerPoint and burn the slide show to a CD. In Windows, just insert a blank CD-R and, from the window that pops up, select the Open Writeable CD folder. Drag the files into the folder and click Write These Files to CD. On a Mac, insert a blank CD-R, select the standard format, and drag the files into the CD icon. Drag the CD icon into the trash can to burn the disc.

8. Design a label and insert for your CD if you wish (if your printable labels didn't come with software to help you do this, search the Internet for templates or freeware you can download).

9. Print your labels and jewel-case inserts and then apply the labels and place the inserts in the cases. Pop in the CDs, and you're ready to share your project.

RELATIONSHIP CHART

What's the difference between a second cousin once removed and a first cousin twice removed? And what the heck does "removed" mean, anyway? Use this relationship chart to sort out the connection between any two people. ("Removed" refers not to how distant a relationship is but the difference in the number of generations between two cousins and their common ancestor: One generation equals one remove.)

Instructions:

1. Identify the most recent common ancestor of the two individuals with the unknown relationship.

2. Determine the common ancestor's relationship to each person (for example, grandparent or great-grandparent).

3. In the topmost row of the chart, find the common ancestor's relationship to cousin number one. In the far-left column, find the common ancestor's relationship to cousin number two.

4. Trace the row and column from step 3. The square where they meet show the two individuals' relationship.

	Parent	Grandparent	Great-Grandparent	Great-great Grandparent
Parent	Siblings	Nephew or Niece	Grandnephew or –niece	Great-grandnephew or –niece
Grandparent	Nephew or Niece	First Cousins	First Cousins Once Removed	First Cousins Twice Removed
Great-Grandparent	Grandnephew or -niece	First Cousins Once Removed	Second Cousins	Second Cousins Once Removed
Great-great Grandparent	Great-grandnephew or -niece	First Cousins Twice Removed	Second Cousins Once Removed	Third Cousins
Third-great Grandparent	Great-great-grandnephew or -niece	First Cousins Three Times Removed	Second Cousins Twice Removed	Third Cousins Once Removed
Fourth-great Grandparent	Third-great-grandnephew or –niece	First Cousins Four Times Removed	Second Cousins Three Times Removed	Third Cousins Twice Removed
Fifth-great Grandparent	Fourth-great-grandnephew or –niece	First Cousins Five Times Removed	Second Cousins Four Times Removed	Third Cousins Three Times Removed
Sixth-great Grandparent	Fifth-great-grandnephew or –niece	First Cousins Six Times Removed	Second Cousins Five Times Removed	Third Cousins Four Times Removed

Third-great Grandparent	Fourth-great Grandparent	Fifth-great Grandparent	Sixth-great Grandparent
Great-great-grand-nephew or - niece	Third-great-grand-nephew or -niece	Fourth-great-grand-nephew or -niece	Fifth-great-grand-nephew or -niece
First Cousins Three Times Removed	First Cousins Four Times Removed	First Cousin Five Time Removed	First Cousins Six Times Removed
Second Cousins Twice Removed	Second Cousins Three Times Removed	Second Cousins Four Times Removed	Second Cousins Five Times Removed
Third Cousins Once Removed	Third Cousins Twice Removed	Third Cousins Three Times Removed	Third Cousins Four Times Removed
Fourth Cousins	Fourth Cousins Once Removed	Fourth Cousins Twice Removed	Fourth Cousins Three Times Removed
Fourth Cousins Once Removed	Fifth Cousins	Fifth Cousins Once Removed	Fifth Cousins Twice Removed
Fourth Cousins Twice Removed	Fifth Cousins Once Removed	Sixth Cousins	Sixth Cousins Once Removed
Fourth Cousins Three Times Removed	Fifth Cousins Twice Removed	Sixth Cousins Once Removed	Seventh Cousins

WEB SITES

Genealogy has become a hugely popular online pastime, thanks to a proliferation of Web sites dedicated to family tree tracing. With so many places to click, where do you start? These are our favorite destinations for beginners—many are recipients of *Family Tree Magazine's* annual 101 Best Web Sites award. (Sites marked with a $ require a fee to access most of their content.)

AfriGeneas

<www.afrigeneas.com> A terrific starting place for those with African-American roots, AfriGeneas has how-to advice, message boards, a surname index, and plenty of records.

American Memory

<memory.loc.gov> Explore American history through the treasures of the Library of Congress. This special site contains 9 million digitized items, including historical documents, photos and maps.

Ancestry.com ($)

<www.ancestry.com> Highlights: free family tree builder, search of users' family trees, message boards, and learning center. The largest source of online genealogy records, including 1790–1930 US census indexes and records, National Archives passenger lists, military records, historical newspapers, and more.

Bureau of Land Management General Land Office Records

<www.glorecords.blm.gov> If your ancestors bought land from the federal government, you'll find the "patent" in this searchable database of millions of land records from 1820 to 1908. (Hint: The records don't cover the 13 colonies and a handful of other states that had no federally owned land.)

Canadian Genealogy Centre

<www.collectionscanada.gc.ca/genealogy/index-e.html> Library and Archives Canada houses all of Canada's federal records. Its genealogy Web site offers research tools and instructions, plus digitized vital records, passenger lists, censuses, and more.

CastleGarden.org

<www.castlegarden.org> If your family arrived in New York before Ellis Island opened in 1892, check this site, named for the city's first immigration station. The database covers 10 million immigrants back to 1830.

Civil War Soldiers & Sailors Database

<www.itd.nps.gov/cwss> Use this database of 6.3 million names as a springboard for finding Civil War ancestors, whether Union or Confederate. Once you identify a soldier, you'll learn about his regiment and battles.

Cyndi's List

<www.cyndislist.com> Think of Cyndi's List as the Yahoo! of genealogy: It categorizes hundreds of thousands of helpful family history Web sites, making it a good first stop to find sites on a wide range of family-history related topics.

Ellis Island

<www.ellisisland.org> More than 40 percent of Americans have a relative who immigrated through Ellis Island's "golden door" between 1892 and 1954. Here you can search the records of the 22 million passengers and crew who came through the famous immigration station by 1924.

Familyrelatives.com ($)

<www.familyrelatives.com> Among this UK site's 600 million original records are birth, marriage,

and death registers; a military collection; censuses of England and Wales; and occupational records. Check the Web site for up-to-date costs for premium content. You can buy one of several pay-per-view plans. FamilyRelatives also offers social networking features—including a community section and photo sharing—for free to registered users.

FamilySearch

<familysearch.org> The Church of Jesus Christ of Latter-Day Saints' genealogy Web site has databases of user-submitted family trees, records indexes, and an extensive how-to library. It continues to digitize and index the millions of microfilmed records. Use the online Family History Catalog for information on renting the rest on microfilm at a local Family History Center.

FamilyTreeMagazine.com

<familytreemagazine.com> Read beginner-friendly how-to articles, access Heritage Toolkits for 40-plus nationalities and ethnicities, ask questions on the forum, watch video demos and library tours, and tune in to a free monthly podcast. For activities to do with kids or help on a school project, visit Family Tree Kids! at *<kids.familytreemagazine.com>*.

Find A Grave

<www.findagrave.com> Perhaps someone has copied details from a family cemetery plot and posted them here. Find A Grave lets you search inscriptions from more than 99 million tombstones worldwide—including many famous people's graves.

Find My Past ($)

<www.findmypast.com> The leading subscription site for UK records offers censuses, civil registrations, military records and emigration passenger lists of ships that left from English ports—including those

that originally set sail from elsewhere. Check the Web site for up-to-date yearly costs, or choose a pay-per-view option. (Price are listed in British Pounds.)

Fold3.com ($)

<www.fold3.com> Fold3 offers free historical photos, colonial government records, Pennsylvania genealogies, New England town records, and a nifty virtual Vietnam Wall. Subscribers can access the 1860 US census, homestead records and Civil War pension records (in progress), Confederate records, Revolutionary War records, naturalizations, and newspapers.

GenealogyBank ($)

<www.genealogybank.com> Subscribers can access historical newspapers; millions of obituaries; old books with military, land, and other records; the American State Papers; and the US Serial Set.

Geni

<www.geni.com> Genealogy newbies will love Geni's slick social-networking-driven family tree builder: You simply start adding in names and information; Geni automatically invites relatives to join via e-mail and searches for ancestral connections in other profiles. Flesh out your tree with photos and videos—it's all free.

GENUKI

<www.genuki.org.uk> Bookmark this must-visit resource for tracing ancestors in England, Ireland, Scotland, Wales, the Channel Islands, and the Isle of Man. The volunteer-run site contains research help, databases, and maps.

HeritageQuest Online

<www.heritagequestonline.com> Ask your public library if it offers remote access to HeritageQuest

Online—if so, you'll be able to connect through the library's Web site for free access to the 1790 to 1930 US censuses, Revolutionary War records, 20,000 family and local history books, and an index to millions of articles published in genealogical journals.

Immigrant Ships Transcribers Guild

<www.immigrantships.net> Before you hunt for microfilm, check here to see if your ancestors' passenger manifest is among the thousands copied and posted here by volunteers.

Interment

<www.interment.net> Like Find A Grave, Interment is an online clearinghouse for millions of cemetery records copied and uploaded by site visitors.

JewishGen

<www.jewishgen.org> Discover an impressive collection of volunteer-generated databases, tools, and reference material to help you explore your Jewish heritage. If you have eastern European ancestors of any ethnicity, try the ShtetLinks to help locate villages back in the old country.

MyHeritage

<www.myheritage.com> This Israel Web site attracts millions with its "what celebrity do you look like?" facial-recognition feature. Genealogy buffs can avail themselves of a free online family tree builder, downloadable software, message boards and a metasearch of hundreds of popular genealogy databases on other Web sites.

Nationwide Gravesite Locator

<gravelocator.cem.va.gov> Looking for a military relative's grave? Search this site for burial locations of veterans and their dependents in national and state military cemeteries.

OneGreatFamily ($)

<www.onegreatfamily.com> This online and offline family tree builder merges together user-submitted pedigrees whose ancestors match—resulting in a "single, unified global family tree." Check the Web site for up-to-date annual costs.

Perry-Castañeda Library Map Collection

<www.lib.utexas.edu/maps> Wherever your ancestors came from, this site likely has a historical map of it. Check for country maps from the time your family lived there to print out and save in this book or save a digital copy to keep with your computer files.

RootsWeb

<www.rootsweb.ancestry.com> Highlights: Genealogy's oldest, largest free Web site, a sister site to Ancestry.com, with which it shares message boards and a database of user-submitted family tree. RootsWeb also serves up thousands of volunteer-created record indexes, e-mail lists, and how-to advice.

TheShipsList

<www.theshipslist.com> Besides searching passenger list data, you can view pictures of ships and steamship-line advertisements to help envision your ancestors' voyage.

TribalPages

<www.tribalpages.com> Search hundreds of thousands of family trees and photos. You also can store family tree data here and create charts and reports.

USGenWeb

<www.usgenweb.org> Log on to the pages for your ancestors' states and counties for how-to tips, historical background, reference material, and goodies such as record indexes and transcriptions. Because it's an all-volunteer effort, each location's contents vary.

WeRelate

<www.werelate.org> Genealogy's equivalent to Wikipedia, WeRelate is based on collaborative content: Create pages for people and places that anyone can add to—kind of like virtual Post-it notes. You can add your knowledge to other people's pages, too.

WorldGenWeb Project

<www.worldgenweb.org> The global counterpart to USGenWeb is a great place to start looking for help tracing your family in foreign lands.

World Vital Records ($)

<www.worldvitalrecords.com> By partnering with various genealogy Web site and publishers, World Vital Records brings together historical newspapers, US and UK vital records, books from Quintin Publications, Genealogical Publishing Company, and archive CD books and more.

PUBLICATIONS AND PUBLISHERS

The publishers listed here produce both general genealogy guidebooks and specialized references, such as record abstracts and indexes, to further your research.

A to ZAX: A Comprehensive Dictionary for Genealogists & Historians by Barbara Jean Evans (Hearthside Press)

American Surnames by Elsdon C. Smith (Genealogical Publishing Co.)

Ancestry's Red Book: American State, County & Town Sources, 3rd revised edition, edited by Alice Eichholz (Ancestry)

Dictionary of American Family Names edited by Patrick Hanks, 3 volumes (Oxford University Press)

Discover Your Family History Online A Step-by-Step Guide to Starting Your Genealogy Search by Nancy Hendrickson (Family Tree Books)

The Everything Family Tree Book: Research and Preserve Your Family History by Kimberly Powell (Adams Media)

The Everything Guide to Online Genealogy: A Complete Resource to Using the Web to Trace Your Family History by Kimberly Powell (Adams Media)

Family History Detective A Step-by-Step Guide to Investigating Your Family Tree by Desmond Walls Allen (Family Tree Books)

Family Photo Detective Learn How to Find Genealogy Clues in Old Photos and Solve Family Photo Mysteries by Maureen A. Taylor (Family Tree Books)

Family Tree Magazine, a bimonthly how-to magazine for discovering, preserving, and celebrating family history, (888) 403-9002 <www.familytreemagazine.com>

Family Tree Pocket Reference from the Editors of Family Tree Magazine (Family Tree Books)

The Family Tree Problem Solver by Marsha Hoffman Rising (Family Tree Books)

The Family Tree Sourcebook by the editors of Family Tree Magazine (Family Tree Books)

From the Family Kitchen Discover Your Food Heritage and Preserve Favorite Recipes by Gena Philibert-Ortega (Family Tree Books)

Genealogical Publishing Company
3600 Clipper Mill Road, Suite 260, Baltimore, MD
21211, (800) 599-9561 *<www.genealogical.com>*

The Genealogist's Census Pocket Reference
From Allison Dolan and the Editors of *Family Tree
Magazine* (Family Tree Books)

The Genealogist's U.S. History Pocket Reference
by Nancy Hendrickson (Family Tree Books)

The Handybook for Genealogists, 11th edition
(Everton Publishers)

Heritage Books
100 Railroad Avenue, Suite 104, Westminster, MD
21157, (800) 876-6103 *<www.heritagebooks.com>*

How to Archive Family Keepsakes by Denise May
Levenick (Family Tree Books)

**Saving Stuff: How to Care for and Preserve
Your Collectibles, Heirlooms, and Other Prized
Possessions** by Don Williams and Louisa Jaggar
(Fireside Press)

**The Source: A Guidebook of American Geneal-
ogy,** 3rd edition, edited by Loretto Dennis Szucs and
Sandra Hargreaves Luebking (Ancestry)

**Unpuzzling Your Past: The Best Selling Basic
Guide to Genealogy,** 4th edition, by Emily Anne
Croom (Betterway Books)

ARCHIVES AND LIBRARIES

You can probably get a good head start on your family
tree at your local library, especially if it has a genealogy
or history section or subscribes to one of the popular

online genealogy services (such as HeritageQuest Online
or Ancestry.com Library Edition). But if you hit a "brick
wall" and need to go beyond what your hometown library has, tap into the resources of these institutions with
national and international genealogical collections.

Allen County Public Library
900 Library Plaza, Fort Wayne, IN 46802
(260) 421-1200
<www.acpl.lib.in.us>

**Clayton Library Center for
Genealogical Research**
5300 Caroline, Houston, TX 77004
(832) 393-2600
<www.houstonlibrary.org/clayton>

**Daughters of the American
Revolution Library**
1776 D Street NW, Washington, DC 20006
(202) 628-1776
<www.dar.org/library>

Family History Library
35 N. West Temple Street, Salt Lake City, UT 84150
(866) 406-1830
<www.familysearch.org>
Visit *<familysearch.org/locations/centerlocator>*
to find locations of Family History research centers.

Godfrey Memorial Library
134 Newfield Street, Middletown, CT 06457
(860) 346-4375
<www.godfrey.org>

Library of Congress
101 Independence Avenue SE, Thomas Jefferson
Building, LJ G42, Washington, DC 20540
<www.loc.gov/rr/genealogy>

Mid-Continent Public Library Midwest Genealogy Center

3440 South Lee's Summit Road, Independence, MO 64055

(816) 252-7228

<*www.mymcpl.org/genealogy*>

US National Archives and Records Administration

8601 Adelphi Road, College Park, MD 20740

(866) 272-6272

<*www.archives.gov*>

Find locations of regional research centers at <*www.archives.gov/locations*>.

New England Historic Genealogical Society Library

99 Newbury Street, Boston, MA 02116

(888) 296-3447

<*www.americanancestors.org*>

New York Public Library

The Irma and Paul Milstein Division of United States History, Local History and Genealogy, Stephen A. Schwarzman Building, Fifth Avenue and 42nd Street, Room 121, New York, NY 10018

(212) 930-0828

<*www.nypl.org/milstein*>

Newberry Library

60 West Walton Street, Chicago, IL 60610

<*www.newberry.org/genealogy-and-local-history*>

Public Library of Cincinnati and Hamilton County

800 Vine Street, Cincinnati, OH 45202

(513) 369-6900

<*www.cincinnatilibrary.org/main/genlocal.html*>

SOCIETIES AND ORGANIZATIONS

Genealogical societies in your area—or in the place your family lived—are often excellent resources for learning. Or you may want to hire a professional researcher to look up information for you in a faraway archive. These national associations can lead you to local societies and researchers.

Association of Professional Genealogists

P.O. Box 350998, Westminster, CO 80035

(303) 465-6980

<*www.apgen.org*>

Board for Certification of Genealogists

P.O. Box 14291, Washington, DC 20044

<*www.bcgcertification.org*>

Federation of Genealogical Societies

PO Box 200940, Austin, TX 78720

(888) 347-1500

<*www.fgs.org*>

National Genealogical Society

3108 Columbia Pike, Suite 300, Arlington, VA 22204

(800) 473-0060

<*www.ngsgenealogy.org*>

SOFTWARE

WINDOWS SOFTWARE

Ancestral Quest

Incline Software, <*www.ancquest.com*>, $29.95; free demo version available

Family Tree Builder

MyHeritage, <*www.myheritage.com/family-tree-builder*>, free

Family Tree Maker
Ancestry.com, *<www.familytreemaker.com>*, $39.99

Genbox Family History
Thoughtful Creations, *<www.genbox.com>*, $29.95; free trial available

Legacy Family Tree Deluxe
Millennia, *<www.legacyfamilytree.com>*, $29.95; free Standard Version

The Master Genealogist, Gold Edition
Wholly Genes Software, *<www.whollygenes.com/tmg.htm>*, $59; free trial available

RootsMagic
RootsMagic, Inc., *<www.rootsmagic.com>*, $29.95; free trial available

MACINTOSH SOFTWARE

GEDitCOM II
shareware by John A. Nairn, *<www.geditcom.com>*, $64.99, free demo version available

iFamily for Leopard
shareware by Keith Wilson, *<www.ifamilyfortiger.com>*, $29.95

Heredis Mac X.2
BSD Concept, *<www.myheredis.com>*, $59.99; Free trial version

MacFamilyTree 51
Synium Software, *<www.synium.de/products/mac-familytree>*, $49; free trial version available

Reunion 10
Leister Productions, *<www.leisterpro.com>*, around $99; free demo available

ARCHIVAL SUPPLIERS

To preserve your family heirlooms for posterity, you can buy the same types of storage supplies museums and libraries use to safeguard their treasures. These companies offer products ranging from acid-free boxes to binders to bridal gown preservation kits.

Archival Methods
235 Middle Road, Henrietta, NY 14467
(866) 877-7050
<www.archivalmethods.com>

Archival Products
P.O. Box 1413, Des Moines, IA 50306
(800) 526-5640
<www.archival.com>

Conservation Resources International
5532 Port Royal Road, Springfield, VA 22151
(800) 634-6932
<www.conservationresources.com>

Gaylord
P.O. Box 4901, Syracuse, NY 13221
(800) 962-9580
<www.gaylordmart.com>

Hollinger Metal Edge
P.O. Box 8360, Fredericksburg, VA 22404
(800) 634-0491
<www.hollingercorp.com>

Light Impressions

2340 Brighton Henrietta Town Line Road, Rochester, NY 14623

(800) 975-6429

<www.lightimpressionsdirect.com>

Masterpak

145 E. 57th St., New York, NY 10022

(800) 922-5522

<www.masterpak-usa.com>

Preservation Station

P.O. Box 447, Occoquan, VA 22125-0447

(571) 230-3777

<www.preservesmart.com>

Talas

330 Morgan Avenue, Brooklyn, NY 11211

(212) 219-0770

<www.talasonline.com>

University Products

517 Main Street, Holyoke, MA 01040

(800) 628-1912

<www.universityproducts.com>

FAMILY TREE WALL CHARTS

Wall charts are perfect for displaying at your family reunion and other large gatherings to show everyone who's who. These wall-chart services offer templated tree designs you can customize with your family's information, the printing of a tree you've designed with your genealogy software, or both. The list also includes sources for decorative fill-in-the-blank charts like the one in this book.

Affordable Portable Pedigree

<http://roots.cs.byu.edu/pedigree>

Ancestor Circles

<www.ancestor-circles.com>

Ancestry Graphics & Printing

26W482 Blair, Winfield, IL 60190

(630) 653-8400

<www.ancestryprinting.com/familytree.html>

Family Chartmasters

P.O. Box 1080, Pleasant Grove, UT 84062

(801) 872-4278

<familychartmasters.com>

Family History Store

Kindred Trails, Inc.,1519 Moses Mountain Rd., Tensed, ID 83870

(866) 874-2223

<www.thefamilyhistorystore.com>

Fampres

Loheweg 5, 91056 Erlangen, Germany

+49 (9135) 7 21 72 04

<www.fampres.com/en>

Fun Stuff for Genealogists

P.O. Box 1167, Mishawaka, IN 46546

(877) 259-6144

<www.funstuffforgenealogists.com>

Genealogy Printers

Genealogy House, 15 Linley Drive, Bushbury, Wolverhampton, WV10 8JJ, United Kingdom

+44 (1902) 836284

Heartland Family Graphics

<www.familygraphics.com>

Keepsake Family Trees by Olsongraphics

2424 South Krameria Street, Denver, CO 80222

(888) 759-4228

<olsonetc.com>

MyCanvas

(800) 507-4612

<www.mycanvas.com>

Paper Tree

<www.grillyourgranny.com>

Pictorial Genealogy

1535 Ford Avenue, Redondo Beach, CA 90278

(310) 379-8221

<www.picgene.com>

Reflections Artistry

23 Ray Drive, Kirksville, MO 63501

(888) 690-0237

<www.reflectionsartistry.com>

Tree Maker

P.O. Box 128, Cedar Hill, TN 37032

(866) 480-0202

<www.thetreemaker.com>

Wholly Genes

5144 Flowertuft Court, Columbia, MD 21044

(877) 864-3264

<www.whollygenes.com>

Ye Olde Genealogie Shoppe

9605 Vandergriff Rd, Indianapolis, IN 46239

(800) 419-0200

<www.yogs.com>

DNA TESTING

Test Types

You've probably heard about DNA tests for genealogy. If you're thinking about getting tested, keep in mind that genetic genealogy is a supplement to traditional research—your results won't reveal your entire family tree dating back centuries. Before you shell out $100 to $300, use this quick guide to become familiar with the scope and limitations of each type of test.

Y-DNA

Because surnames, like Y chromosomes, are passed from father to son, a Y-DNA test can be a useful tool in determining whether families with the same last name are related—but it can't pinpoint the common ancestor. Because only males receive the Y chromosome, only men can take this test. Females who want to find out more about their paternal line need to have a male relative from that line tested.

Mitochondrial DNA

Somewhat like the feminine version (with a few differences) of the Y-DNA test, a mitochondrial (mt) DNA test will tell you about your female line with no influence of any males along that line. This test is best for telling you about your "deep" maternal-line ancestry—you'll be assigned to a haplogroup, often described as your branch of the world family tree. MtDNA passes from mother to both sons and daughters, so men and women can take this test.

Ethnic

To discover your ethnic ancestry, you'll need to take a standard Y-DNA or mtDNA test through a lab that can provide additional analysis comparing your results to those typical of certain ethnicities. You'll have to be mindful about choosing the correct family member to test. If you think your mother's father was American Indian, for example, don't test yourself—your mother didn't get Y-DNA or mtDNA from him, and neither did you. Instead have her brother take a Y-DNA test.

Biogeographical

Also called admixture tests, these examine autosomal DNA markers to determine your genetic heritage among anthropological groups such as Native American, Indo-European, east Asian and Sub-Saharan African. Additional testing can further subdivide certain groups. These tests are somewhat controversial because results can be inconclusive, and the east Asian and Native American groups can be hard to differentiate.

Autosomal or Short Tandem Repeat (STR)

The best way to confirm if you're related to a living person is with an STR test. It can determine what relationship (if any), such as parent and child, sibling or cousin, exists between two individuals. Both individuals must provide a DNA sample.

TESTING COMPANIES

23andMe

<*www.23andme.com*>, help@23andme.com. Tests offered: autosomal; results include tools for interpreting test results relating to health information and deep ancestry

African Ancestry

<*www.africanancestry.com*>, (202) 723-0900. Tests offered: ethnic (African)

AfricanDNA

<*www.africandna.com*>, (713) 868-1438. Tests offered: ethnic (African; can also order genealogical research services)

Ancestry DNA

<*dna.ancestry.com*> Tests offered: mtDNA, Y-DNA

Chromosomal Laboratories

<*www.chromosomallabs.com/ancestry.html*> (877) 434-0292. Tests offered: Y-DNA, mtDNA

DNA Consultants

<*www.dnaconsultants.com*>, (505) 473-5155. Tests offered: biogeographical, Y-DNA, mtDNA, ethnic (Native American and African-American)

DNA Heritage

<*www.dnaheritage.com*>, (888) 806-2588. Tests offered: Y-DNA, mtDNA

Family Tree DNA

<*www.familytreedna.com*>, (713) 868-1438. Tests offered: Y-DNA, mtDNA, biogeographical, ethnic (Native American, African-American, Jewish), STR

Identigene

<*www.dnatesting.com*>, (888) 404-4343. Tests offered: STR

National Geographic Genographic Project

<*genographic.nationalgeographic.com*> Tests offered: mtDNA, Y-DNA (12 markers only)

Oxford Ancestors

<*oxfordancestors.com*>, +44 (0)845 5438060. Tests offered: mtDNA, Y-DNA, ethnic (British Isles and others)

WHERE TO LOOK FOR RECORDS

If you want to start exploring historical records of your family, here's where to check first for commonly used genealogical records.

US CENSUSES
- Ancestry.com and Ancestry.com Library Edition (searchable on any name)
- HeritageQuest Online (searchable by head of household)
- US National Archives and Records Administration and its regional branches
- Family History Library and its local research centers
- Genealogical libraries

VITAL RECORDS
Birth, marriage, death, divorce—see the chart on the next for the dates when state-level record keeping began.
- State vital-statistics offices (for recent records)
- State archives or libraries (for older records)
- County courthouse or vital-statistics office
- Town halls (in New England)
- Family History Library and its local research centers
- Genealogical libraries

MILITARY RECORDS
- Ancestry.com and Ancestry.com Library Edition
- Fold3.com
- US National Archives and Records Administration and its regional branches (copies can be ordered online at *<http://archives.gov/order>*)
- Family History Library and its local research centers
- State archives

PASSENGER LISTS
- Ellis Island and Castle Garden Web sites for New York arrivals
- Ancestry.com and Ancestry Library Edition
- US National Archives and Records Administration and its regional branches
- Family History Library and its local research centers
- State archives
- Genealogical libraries
- World Vital Records

NATURALIZATION AND CITIZENSHIP PAPERS
- Family History Library and its local research centers
- Local, county, and state courthouses
- US Citizenship and Immigration Services (after 1906 only)
- Fold3.com

LAND AND PROPERTY RECORDS
- County courthouses (deeds)
- Bureau of Land Management General Land
- Office Records Web site (for purchases of federal land)
- US National Archives and Records Administration and its regional branches
- State archives
- Genealogical libraries

WILLS AND PROBATE FILES
- County courthouses
- Family History Library and its local research centers
- State archives

VITAL RECORDS CHART

Take note of the years that statewide vital record-keeping officially began in each US state—that's when countries started to collect birth, marriage, and death information and report it to state offices. Some counties or towns kept stats earlier, and some were slow to comply with state laws, so check with your ancestors' local government for record availability.

	Birth Records	Marriage Records	Death Records
Alabama	1908	1936	1908
Alaska	1913	1913	1913
Arizona	1909	1909	1909
Arkansas	1914	1917	1914
California	1905	1905	1905
Colorado	1907	1907	1907
Connecticut	1897	1897	1897
Delaware*	1861	1847	1881
District of Columbia**	1874	1811	1874
Florida	1899	1927	1899
Georgia	1919	1952	1919
Hawaii	1842	1842	1859
Idaho	1911	1947	1911
Illinois	1916	1962	1916
Indiana	1907	1958	1899
Iowa	1880	1880	1880
Kansas	1911	1913	1911
Kentucky	1911	1958	1911
Louisiana***	1914	none	1914
Maine	1892	1892	1892
Maryland	1898	1950	1898
Massachusetts	1841	1841	1841
Michigan	1867	1867	1867
Minnesota	1900	1958	1908
Mississippi	1912	1926	1912
Missouri	1910	1881	1910

	Birth Records	Marriage Records	Death Records
Montana	1907	1943	1907
Nebraska	1905	1909	1905
Nevada	1911	1968	1911
New Hampshire	1901	1901	1901
New Jersey	1848	1848	1848
New Mexico	1920	1920	1920
New York	1880	1880	1880
North Carolina	1913	1962	1913
North Dakota	1907	1925	1907
Ohio	1908	1949	1908
Oklahoma	1908	1908	1908
Oregon	1903	1906	1903
Pennsylvania	1906	1885	1906
Rhode Island	1853	1853	1853
South Carolina	1915	1950	1915
South Dakota	1905	1905	1905
Tennessee****	1908	1945	1908
Texas	1903	1966	1903
Utah	1905	1887	1905
Vermont	1955	1955	1955
Virginia	1912	1912	1912
Washington	1907	1968	1907
West Virginia	1917	1964	1917
Wisconsin	1907	1907	1907
Wyoming	1909	1941	1909
Missouri	1910	1881	1910

*Delaware's statewide birth and death records stop in 1863 and resume in 1881.

**District of Columbia did not file death records during the Civil War.

***All Louisiana Birth Records are kept in parish clerk offices.

****Tennessee has no statewide birth or death records for 1913.

FAMILY
TREE
BOOKS

An imprint of Penguin Random House LLC

penguinrandomhouse.com

Copyright © 2009 and 2013 by Penguin Random House LLC

Penguin supports copyright. Copyright fuels creativity, encourages diverse voices, promotes free speech, and creates a vibrant culture. Thank you for buying an authorized edition of this book and for complying with copyright laws by not reproducing, scanning, or distributing any part of it in any form without permission. You are supporting writers and allowing Penguin to continue to publish books for every reader.

ISBN 978-1-4403-3062-9

Printed in the United States of America

11th Printing

PUBLISHER/EDITORIAL DIRECTOR: Allison Dolan
EDITOR: Jacqueline Musser
DESIGNER: Elyse Schwanke